CHEEKY MONKEY

HiLARiOUS JOKES, PUNS, RiDDLES & PRANKS

Cheeky Monkey - Hilarious Jokes, Puns, Riddles & Pranks
© 2024 by Better Day Books, an imprint of Schiffer Publishing, Ltd.

Publisher: Peg Couch
Book Designer: Michael Douglas
Editor: Colleen Dorsey

Illustrations throughout the book are credited to their respective creators via Creative Market: animal illustration packages copyright CreativeCatandCo; "Font Bundle" and "Tropicana" packages copyright AngelinaKovel

Library of Congress Control Number: 2024934588

ISBN: 978-0-7643-6867-7
Printed in China
10 9 8 7 6 5 4 3 2 1

Published by Better Day Books, an imprint of Schiffer Publishing, Ltd.

Better Day Books
Email:
hello@betterdaybooks.com
Web:
www.betterdaybooks.com
Visit us on Instagram!
@better_day_books

Schiffer Publishing
4880 Lower Valley Road
Atglen, PA 19310
Phone: 610-593-1777
Fax: 610-593-2002
Email:
info@schifferbooks.com
Web:
www.schifferbooks.com

For our complete selection of fine books on this and related subjects, please visit our website at www.betterdaybooks.com. You may also write for a free catalog.

Better Day Books titles are available at special discounts for bulk purchases for sales promotions or premiums. Special editions, including personalized covers, corporate imprints, and excerpts, can be created in large quantities for special needs. For more information, contact the publisher.

CHEEKY MONKEY

HiLARiOUS JOKES, PUNS, RiDDLES & PRANKS

A Tickle-Your-Funny-Bone Book for Silly Kids Who Love to LOL

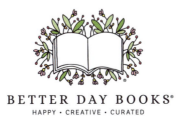

BETTER DAY BOOKS®

HAPPY · CREATIVE · CURATED

CONTENTS

ACTIVITIES

Look for these special Cheeky Monkey Activities scattered throughout the book!

WELCOME!

Are you ready to become a cheeky monkey? You'll be cracking up your friends and family in no time with this ultimate joke book designed especially for first-time jokesters!

Packed with tons of jokes, riddles, puns, and bonus activities, this super-cute book delivers endless giggles for kids and parents alike, creating cherished memories with every page. The clever Rate My Joke system (more details on that when you turn the page!) not only adds an extra layer of fun but also encourages deeper interactions between the jokester (that's you!) and the audience, making time shared with this book a true bonding experience.

This book is also a valuable tool for expanding creativity, helping you develop your performance skills and your sense of humor. With each joke and riddle, the book acts as a vocabulary booster, ensuring that the fun is both contagious and educational.

So get ready to spread smiles and happiness as you embark on a joyful journey of laughter!

HOW TO USE THIS BOOK

This book includes:

200+ jokes

100+ riddles

Special Cheeky Monkey Activities to fill out

And a super-fun Rate My Joke system!

When it comes to the jokes and riddles, you can really use the book however you'd like. You can read an entire page of jokes or riddles to your audience, or you can pass the book around and tell one joke per person. You can pick pages at random or go in order. It's totally up to you!

On the facing page, you'll find the Rate My Joke key! Every time you tell a joke or a riddle, after you've delivered the punch line or solution, ask your audience to rate it using this key. The Rate My Joke key is printed on the inner front and back flaps too so you can always easily find it and show it to your audience. If you want to keep track of what your audience thinks of your jokes on a separate piece of paper, go for it!

Also scattered throughout the book are Cheeky Monkey Activities in which you get to answer fun questions and participate in writing your own jokes. You'll also find ideas for fun (and harmless) pranks you can pull on your unwitting friends and family!

**You're going to have so much fun.
Now get out there and be a cheeky monkey!**

AM i A CHEEKY MONKEY?

Roared with laughter

You're a cheeky monkey!

That's so clever!

You make me smile

I feel half and half

That's a stretch

I don't get it

I can do better

That's bananas!

RATE MY JOKE

HOW TO BE A COMEDiAN

A great joke is not simply the words on the page—part of it is the performance of the joke! Imagine the difference between a robot reciting a joke and a comedian telling a joke. You want to be the comedian, not the robot! Follow these tips to become a true master of comedy. You'll have your audience rolling on the floor laughing in no time!

READ THE WHOLE JOKE FIRST: Before you say the joke or pose the riddle, read what the answer is to yourself. This will help you think about how best to say the joke—like where to put the emphasis in the sentence.

USE YOUR VOICE: If you have a big audience, make sure to project so that everyone can hear you! If you're talking to just one person, still make sure to use an interesting and engaging voice. Exaggerate the words as you say them as if you were a circus announcer or a radio host.

TAKE YOUR TIME: Don't rush through reading a joke or riddle. You want your audience to understand what you say the first time you say it! Similarly, don't rush through pages and pages of jokes as fast as possible. Chat about each joke and use the Rate My Joke key before moving on to a new joke.

USE YOUR FACE AND HANDS: Add suspense and fun by really hamming it up with facial expressions and hand motions. Humor is not just in the words! If space allows, stand up to deliver your joke like a true comedian performing on a stage.

GIVE 'EM A CHANCE: Give you audience a chance to try to figure out the joke or riddle after you say it! For riddles especially, let them talk through their logic and ideas and try to come up with an answer. Don't ruin their fun by blurting out the answer before they're ready!

A DIFFERENT APPROACH: If you want to try to guess the answer to a riddle or a joke at the same time as your audience, simply don't read the answer ahead of time! Then, when everyone is ready, flip the book over and reveal the punch line.

BE KIND: Comedy is about laughter, not putting people down! If someone can't figure out a riddle or doesn't understand a joke, take that as an opportunity for learning and don't make fun of the other person.

MATCH YOUR JOKES TO YOUR AUDIENCE: Considering the audience is key to landing a hilarious joke. Pick out jokes that will make sense to your audience or are about topics that they like. So, for example, if your friend loves animals, pick out some cat or cow jokes!

SHARE: Don't hog the book! There's a reason open-mic nights are so popular—it's tons of fun to give lots of people the chance to be a comedian. Everyone has a different style, voice, and comedy taste. So pass the book around and let everyone join in!

HA
HA

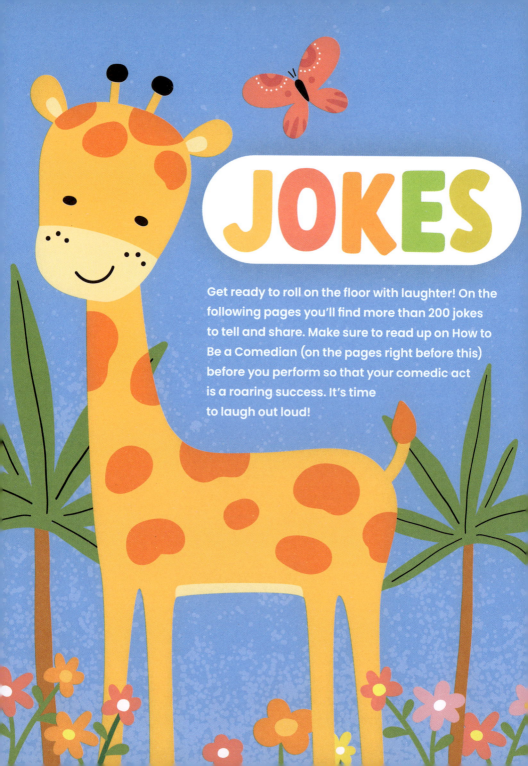

JOKES

Get ready to roll on the floor with laughter! On the following pages you'll find more than 200 jokes to tell and share. Make sure to read up on How to Be a Comedian (on the pages right before this) before you perform so that your comedic act is a roaring success. It's time to laugh out loud!

Which meal is the astronaut's favorite?

There's a boy in a car wearing a blue shirt. What's his name?

How did the barber win the race?

Why can't Elsa walk the dog?

Why was the golfer wearing two sets of pants?

How does a hurricane see?

How does the paint store staff answer the phone?

....

What do you say if someone tries to eat your cheese?

....

If April showers bring May flowers, what do May flowers bring?

....

What's a tornado's favorite game to play at a party?

....

What do you call a sad berry?

....

Why was the banana sent to the doctor?

....

ANSWERS: Yellow / Nacho cheese! / Pilgrims / Twister / A blueberry / Because it wasn't peeling good

14

....
....
....
....

What did the nose tell the finger?

What kind of shoes do stealthy ninjas wear?

....
....
....
....

What country is the fastest?

....
....
....
....

What do you call a factory that makes products that are just okay?

When does the moon decide it has had enough?

Where does a superhero buy food?

How many pears grow on a tree?

What did one flag say to the other?

What can't hear even though it has several ears?

WHY DiD THE APPLE STOP?

What does a cow prefer
to drink?

....

What do you call the
scariest plant?

....

What is a witch's favorite
subject at school?

....

Why did the smartphone
wear glasses?

....

What is a skeleton's
favorite instrument?

....

Why do genies
go to therapy?

....

ANSWERS: A s-moo-thie / Bam-boo / Spelling / It lost its contacts /
A trom-bone / They have too many bottled-up feelings

18

What did the angry
mummy do?

What is blue and doesn't
weigh much?

Which genre of music
do balloons dislike?

What did the baseball glove
say to the ball?

How do seas and oceans
say hello?

What do you call a toaster that
works in an amusement park?

LAUGH-OUT-LOUD WORDS

There are so many words to learn in the English language, and some of them are downright hilarious to use and say! Let's take a look at a few and also see if you can come up with any of your own favorites!

Words That Mean "Funny"

When you're reading, listening to, and laughing at jokes, instead of saying, "That's funny!" every single time, try to use some of these different words that also mean funny!

HiLARiOUS   **AMUSiNG**

HYSTERiCAL   **COMEDiC**

SiDE-SPLiTTiNG   **RiB-TiCKLiNG**

COMiCAL   **LOL-WORTHY**

PRiCELESS

Silly Words with Silly Meanings!

+ **Hullabaloo:** this noun means a lot of unorganized noise and activity

+ **Flibbertigibbet:** this noun means a person who is silly and not able to be serious

+ **Redonkulous:** this is a wacky pronunciation of the adjective "ridiculous," which means silly or unbelievable

+ **Hoity-toity:** this adjective means someone or something that is stuck up or fancy

+ **Whippersnapper:** this noun means someone younger than you who has a lot of attitude!

+ **Bamboozle:** this verb means to scam or trick someone

+ **Scrumdiddlyumptious:** this adjective means extremely delicious

+ **Gobbledygook:** this noun means words or sentences that are nonsense or gibberish (which is another a silly word!)

+ **Kerfuffle:** this noun means a disturbance, usually related to an argument

+ **Pumpernickel:** this noun is a type of tasty brown bread!

+ **Higgledy-piggledy:** this adverb means doing something in a messy or disorganized way

Now list some of YOUR favorite silly words and what they mean!

_____

_____

Now poll your friends and family! What are their favorite silly words?

_____

_____

How do cats bake a cake?

....
....
....
....

What did the mom flower say to the little flower?

....
....
....
....

Why should you not talk to circles?

....
....
....
....

Why did the boy toss a clock from the window?

What do you do when astronauts are upset?

Why did the pony get sent to his room?

What has four wheels and flies?

What kind of fish swims only at night?

What do lawyers wear to court?

ANSWERS: Because he wanted to see time fly / Give them some space / He wouldn't stop horse-ing around / A garbage truck / A starfish / Lawsuits

What did the Dalmatian say
after eating lunch?

What kind of food is
never on time?

What kind of key
opens a banana?

What do you call a dog
with a fever?

What has eight eyes
but cannot see?

What kind of space
never goes forward?

ANSWERS: That hit the spot! / Choco-late / A monkey /
A hot dog / Four blind mice / Backspace / (facing page) The Baa-hamas

Where is a cow's favorite place to go?

What always falls in the winter but is never hurt?

What skill do cats excel at?

Why are hockey players such successful bankers?

Why does Santa no longer dare to enter a chimney?

What do you call a rat's brother?

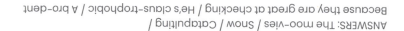

ANSWERS: The moo-vies / Snow / Catapulting / Because they are great at checking / He's claus-trophobic / A bro-dent

Ms. Yellow lives in the yellow house and Mr. Green lives in the green house. Who lives in the white house?

What sits at the bottom of the sea and twitches?

What's a cow's favorite rock?

Why did the girl spread
peanut butter on the road?

What do you call a
running turkey?

What did the triangle say
to the circle?

Following their team's defeat, what
did the carrot say to the salad?

What did the mother bread
say to her child?

Why couldn't the koala
enter the competition?

(facing page) It was having a hare day

ANSWERS: To go with the traffic jam / Fast food / You're pointless /
You have lettuce down / I loaf you / He did not koala-fy /

28

WHY DID THE RABBIT WEAR A HAT?

What do you get when a cow and a trampoline cross paths?

What store does Cupid get his arrows from?

What do you call a wizard that uses ice magic?

Why did the lion cross the road?

What's the best food to eat in the winter?

What bear has no teeth?

What do you call a cow
with only two legs?

Why are ghosts
bad liars?

What do you call
an angry dessert?

What did the bald eagle
get for his birthday?

Why do bees have
sticky hair?

What do you call an
alligator in a vest?

COMPLETE THE STORY

Get ready to tell your own wacky, zany story! For this activity, you will need one person, the "reader," to hold the book and ask for a word to fill each blank, and one person, the "speaker," who will give a word for each blank—without looking at the book page! The reader should write the word down in each blank as they go. At the end, the reader reads the entire story aloud and everyone can see what happened!

If you're the speaker who is coming up with words, try to think of fun, interesting, and unrelated words so that the story turns out as silly as possible!

Each blank in the story will need a word of a different specific type. Below is a refresher of the types of speech, in case you need it!

✦ **Noun:** a person, place, or thing (for example, "computer")

✦ **Verb:** an action word (for example, "babysit")

✦ **Adjective:** a word that describes a noun (for example, "yellow")

My Silly Story

There once was a _____ [noun] named Cheeky who lived in a _____ [adjective] house in the countryside but who never, ever went outside. She was afraid of all the scary _____ [plural noun] that were out there in the big, wide world.

One day, she heard a _____ [noun: a sound] at her door. When she opened it, she saw that it was _____ [noun: a person you know]!

"I've come to take you to _____ [noun: a place] so we can _____ [verb] and eat some yummy _____ [noun: a food]," the visitor said.

"That does sound like a lot of fun, but I'm nervous about leaving my house!" Cheeky said. She asked, "If I come with you, will you protect me from all the _____ [adjective] _____ [plural noun] out there?"

"Of course," the visitor answered. "I always bring a _____ [noun] with me, so I can take care of anyone and anything that bothers us!"

"Okay," Cheeky said. "Let me just grab my _____ [noun]!"

And so Cheeky and her new friend went off to have a _____ [adjective] time together, and Cheeky learned that the big, wide world out past her door was pretty awesome after all.

When a vampire and a snowman meet, what do you get?

What do you give a sick lemon?

Why did the girl run to her bed so quickly?

What do you call a dinosaur with a big vocabulary?

What kind of tree can fit in your hand?

Where can you find a whale that plays the flute?

ANSWERS: Frostbite / Lemon-aid / Because she was trying to catch up on her sleep / A thesaurus / A palm tree / In an orca-stra

Why did the math book
look so sad?

Can a dog jump higher than
the Eiffel Tower?

What do you call
a sleeping bull?

What did the zero say
to the eight?

What do you call a pig
that knows karate?

Where do fish keep
their money?

ANSWERS: Because it had so many problems /
Of course it can—the Eiffel Tower can't jump! / A bulldozer /
I like your belt! / A pork-chop / In the riverbank

Why did the gum
cross the road?

Why did the picture
go to jail?

How do you keep an elephant
from charging?

What do you call a dog
that can tell time?

What do you need to get
to high school?

What did one hat say
to the other hat?

ANSWERS: It was stuck to the chicken's foot / Because it was framed /
Take away its credit card / A watch-dog / A ladder /
Stay put—I'm going on ahead / (facing page) Sham-boo

After he found electricity, how did Benjamin Franklin feel?

Why was the instructor wearing sunglasses?

Which side of a turkey has the most feathers?

Why do strings never win races?

What do spiders do on the internet?

Why did the cookie go to the doctor?

38

What did one plate say to the other?

How do you make a lemon drop?

Which hand is better to write with?

What is a golfer's
favorite number?

What did the traffic light
say to the car?

Why did the chicken cross
the playground?

What did the frog order
for dinner?

What kind of haircuts
do bees get?

How can you tell if someone
is a good farmer?

ANSWERS: Fore / Please don't look—I'm changing / To get to the other slide / Fries and a diet croak / Buzz cuts / They are outstanding in their field / (facing page) Because the players kept dribbling on it

WHY WAS THE BASKETBALL COURT WET?

What kind of school does
ice cream go to?

What do you call a monkey
who loves to dance?

Why did the
computer sneeze?

Why did the student eat
their homework?

What did the diner say when he
ate some shredded cheese?

Why is a calendar
always nervous?

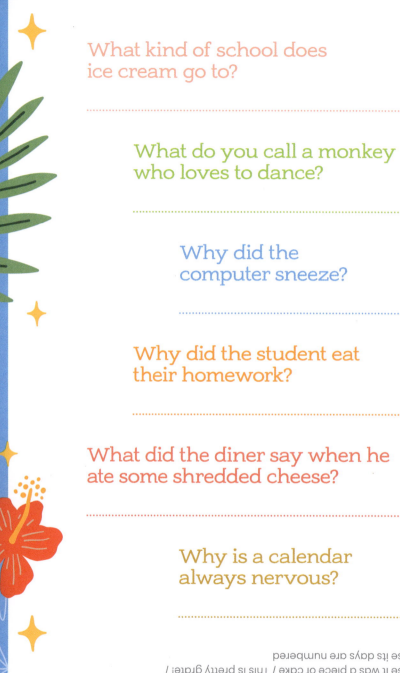

What do you call two
banana peels?

How do scientists make
their breath fresh?

Why do birds fly south
in the winter?

What's a bird's favorite
school subject?

Why is it dangerous to play cards
in the jungle?

Why do seagulls fly
over the sea?

CAPTION THIS

What on earth is going on here? It's time to use your imagination to come up with some funny explanations and stories for what is happening in these three images! Use what you've learned about comedy through this book to imagine something funny to say for each scenario. You can also challenge friends or family to come up with their own captions and then vote on whose caption is the funniest!

This looks fun! What's happening here? _____

_____

_____

_____

Can you believe this? These animals are . . . _____

_____

_____

_____

Where are these best buds headed off to? _____

_____

_____

_____

What do fish play on the piano?

....
....
....
....

What's a math teacher's favorite place?

....
....
....
....

Which language do billboards speak?

....
....
....

What subject do snakes
like to study?

....

What day of the week are
most twins born on?

....

What do you call a fly
with no wings?

....

Why didn't the teddy bear
order dessert?

....

What's a shark's
favorite game?

....

Why did the fishermen
play baseball?

....

Why did Humpty Dumpty have a great fall?

How do you stop a bull from charging?

What is a frog's favorite year?

What is brown and sticky?

What is black and white and looks like a zebra?

What do you call babies in the army?

ANSWERS: To make up for his miserable summer / You unplug it / A leap year / A stick / A zebra / Infant-ry / (facing page) They are always spotted

What did the egg say when breakfast was running late?

....

Who won the princesses' 100-meter dash?

....

What is a cat's favorite color?

....

What's green and smells like blue paint?

....

What do you call a cat burrito?

....

Why don't scientists trust atoms?

....

ANSWERS: Sorry, I have to scramble! / Rapunzel, by a hair / Purr-ple / Green paint / A purr-ito / Because they make up everytyhing!

50

How do you know if there's a giraffe under your bed?

Why did the meteorologist call in sick?

Where can you find a car with no gas?

51

What's the opposite
of high stakes?

....

What treat always makes
a dog laugh?

....

What do cows
order from?

....

What is more threatening
than a tiger?

....

How did the man feel
when the clock broke?

....

When are
cooks mean?

....

WHAT SCHOOL DOES A CARPENTER ATTEND?

Why was the watchdog spinning around and around?

···
···
···
···

What do you call a sausage that always gets its way?

···
···
···
···

What's the smartest insect?

···
···
···
···

What is gray and has big ears,
four legs, a tail, and a trunk?

Where do sharks like to
go on vacation?

Why does a baby pig
eat so much?

Why should you take
a ruler to bed?

If ten dogs run after one dog,
what time is it?

What's the best way
to catch a fish?

MY HiLARiOUS LiFE

Everyone's life is full of laughter, even if you don't realize it! Fill out the answers to these questions about what's funny in your life. This is also a great activity to do aloud with buddies. Maybe you'll learn something about your friends or yourself!

Who is the funniest person you know?

_____

_____

_____

What's the funniest thing a friend ever did?

_____

_____

_____

What's the funniest show you watch?

_____

_____

_____

What is guaranteed to make you laugh?

_____

_____

_____

What's the funniest animal, in your opinion?

_____

_____

_____

When was the last time you peed your pants or fell down laughing?

_____

_____

_____

Have you ever had an uncontrollable fit of laughter during class?

_____

_____

_____

What's your favorite funny movie?

_____

_____

_____

Describe an inside joke you have with someone.

_____

_____

_____

What is your favorite joke in this book?

_____

_____

_____

What do you get if you put a mother duck and six ducklings into a box?

What's the first thing that happens when a kid jumps into a lake?

What are King Kong's favorite cookies?

What kind of ears do engines have?

What is the difference between a tuna fish and a piano?

Why did the woman go outside with her purse open?

Where is a sneeze usually pointed?

Which fish is the most famous?

Why is a traffic cop the strongest person in the world?

How did the cat ace
the test at school?

Which knight created the
round table?

How do you look at
a hippo's teeth?

Why are fish
so smart?

When is a sheepdog most
likely to go into a house?

What kind of a dot
can dance?

What do you call a cat
who drinks lemonade?

What is a bunny's favorite
kind of music?

What happens when a giant
walks through your garden?

Why was Cinderella so bad
at soccer?

Why was the
book cold?

What do you call a
sleeping dinosaur?

ANSWERS: A sourpuss / Hip-hop / All your vegetables turn to squash / She always ran away from the ball / It lost its jacket / A dino-snore

What is the hardest kind of bean
to grow on a farm?

Why did the sun
go to school?

How do you make
a banana shake?

Where does a dog
keep its car?

Why does a giraffe have
such a long neck?

Why do bees hum?

ANSWERS: Jelly beans / To get brighter / Take it to a scary movie /
In a barking lot / Because its head is so far from its body /
Because they don't know the words

What's the worst season of the year for tightrope walkers?

Why is a bucket like a person getting a suntan?

How do you make antifreeze?

How does an astronaut throw a party?

What should you do if you catch a cat eating your dictionary?

Why are comedians terrible chefs?

ANSWERS: The fall / They're both a little pale / Take away her blanket / They planet / Take the words right out of its mouth / Because everything they cook tastes funny / (facing page) it over-swept

WHY WAS THE BROOM LATE FOR ITS APPOINTMENT?

What did the pillowcase say
when the pillow needed help?

What kind of music
do planets sing?

Why don't skeletons
fight each other?

Why are fish so
easy to weigh?

What do you call a can opener
that doesn't work?

Why was the
computer cold?

ANSWERS: Don't worry—I've got you covered! / Neptunes /
They don't have the guts / They have their own scales /
A can't opener / It had left its Windows open

What do you call a train carrying bubblegum?

Why don't Christmas trees knit their own sweaters?

Why was the salad gold?

RIDDLES

Are you ready to give your brain a workout? On the following pages you'll find more than 100 riddles to make you think. Sometimes a riddle may have more than one answer, so if someone gives an answer that is an accurate response to the question, you can consider that a correct answer even if it's not the answer listed in this book. Have fun stumping your friends, family, and maybe even yourself!

If there are three rocks and you take away two, how many do you have?

What can you hold in your left hand but not your right?

What can you catch but not throw?

What has legs but cannot walk?

How many sides does a circle have?

What kind of cup never holds liquid?

What gets bigger when
more is taken away?

Where can you find
an ocean but no water?

What has 18 legs and
catches flies?

What is full of keys but cannot
unlock anything?

What has a tail and a
head but no body?

What is one day away
but never arrives?

Luca's mother had three kids:
Toni, John, and ... ?

What has a ring but no finger?

What occurs once in every minute,
twice in every moment, and yet
never in a thousand years?

What five-letter word gets shorter
if you add two letters to the end?

What can honk without
using a horn?

What has a round head
but no arms or legs?

What has one foot on each side
and one foot in the middle?

What has teeth but
cannot eat?

What has 200 legs
and no feet?

What do you get when
you drop a pumpkin?

What is always answered even
though it has no questions?

Which month has
28 days in it?

ANSWERS: A yardstick / A comb / 100 pairs of pants / Squash /
A doorbell / Every month / (facing page) The temperature (or a staircase!)

What has the head of a cat and the tail of a cat but is not a cat?

What is tall when it's young and short when it's old?

Who always goes to sleep with shoes on?

What falls in winter but never gets hurt?

Which is heavier, a ton of rocks or a ton of feathers?

What has no legs but always runs?

ANSWERS: A kitten / A candle / A horse / Snow / Neither—they weigh the same / A river

What bus crossed
the ocean?

What fish costs
the most?

What has many eyes
but never blinks?

What has a spine
but no bones?

What is full of holes
but holds water?

What will break if you
don't keep it?

ANSWERS: Columbus / A goldfish / A potato /
A book / A sponge / A promise

FiNiSH THiS JOKE

New jokes are surprisingly hard to come up with! Sometimes it helps if someone starts them for you. Now that you've had some practice telling jokes, why not try to write some yourself? Fill in the punch lines with something you think makes sense and is funny for each of these joke setups!

If you can't think of a good punchline with the setups provided, change the nouns that are in the jokes to something else. For example, instead of "Why did the farmer cross the road?," change "farmer" to something else!

You can also use this opportunity to rewrite any joke in the book that you didn't think was funny enough. Can you do better?

Knock, knock.
Who's there?
A cheeky monkey.
A cheeky monkey who?

_____

_____

What did the penguin say to the parrot?

_____

_____

_____

A tiger and a dentist walk into a playground.

_____

What is something you might say both in a library and at an amusement park?

_____

Why did the farmer cross the road?

_____

_____

Why is a city a lot like a baseball?

_____

_____

I like my tacos like I like my clothing:

_____

Write your own complete joke from scratch!
Or rewrite a joke from this book to make it better.

_____

_____

_____

A butcher is 5 feet tall and wears size 10 shoes. What does he weigh?

What goes all around a city but never goes inside?

What can fill a room but takes up no space?

Where was the Declaration of Independence signed?

What is easy to lift but hard to throw?

Who is bigger: Mr. Bigger or Mr. Bigger's baby?

ANSWERS: Meat, of course / A street / Light / At the bottom / A feather / Mr. Bigger's baby—he's a little bigger!

What has more feet in winter than in summer?

The more you take, the more you leave behind. What am I?

What makes it harder to see the more there is?

What kind of room has no doors, windows, floor, or ceiling?

What has a tongue but can't speak?

What has a face and two hands but no arms or legs?

ANSWERS: An ice-skating rink / Footsteps / Darkness / A mushroom / A shoe / A clock

79

What runs around a playground
but never moves?

What 10-letter word
starts with gas?

How can you make
pants last?

What weighs nothing
but cannot be held?

What do you call a very,
very young robin?

What has a neck and
two arms but no head?

ANSWERS: A fence / Automobile / Make all the other clothing first /
Air / An egg / A shirt / (facing page) Are you asleep?

WHICH QUESTION CAN YOU NEVER ANSWER "YES" TO?

What kind of balls
cannot bounce?

What do you fill with
empty hands?

What is at the end
of lunch?

Which is faster:
heat or cold?

What bird is
always sad?

What goes round and round
but never leaves its place?

ANSWERS: Eyeballs / Mittens / The letter "h" / Heat—you can catch a cold / A blue jay / A washing machine

What needs to be answered
but never has a question?

What's the easiest way to
double your money?

What falls down but
can't get up?

What must you break
before you can use it?

What belongs to you but
is used more by others?

What do you bury
while it's alive?

ANSWERS: A phone / Fold it in half / Rain / An egg /
Your name / A plant (or a seed)

83

What is always ahead of you
but cannot be seen?

What will crack if you drop it
but always smiles back when
you smile at it?

What gets wetter
the more it dries?

What disappears as soon
as you mention it?

What goes up but
never comes down?

What has sharp teeth
but does not bite?

ANSWERS: The future / A mirror / A towel /
Silence / Your age / A saw / (facing page) In the dictionary

What can go through a window
but not break it?

....

What has one eye
but cannot see?

....

What two things can never
be eaten for breakfast?

....

What flies all day but
never goes anywhere?

....

What gets rid of mistakes
but never makes them?

....

How long
is a shoe?

....

ANSWERS: Light / A sewing needle / Lunch and dinner /
A flag / An eraser / A foot long

86

What's the difference between
a nickel and a penny?

What is white when dirty
and black when clean?

What can make two
people out of one?

What word is always
pronounced wrong?

What is always served at
dinner but never eaten?

What has hands
but can't clap?

PRANK iDEAS

It is so satisfying to successfully pull a prank on someone! A prank is a practical joke or a mischievous act that you do in secret and that someone else discovers as a surprise. You could pull a prank on anyone, but it's best to reserve pranks for people who know you well and who love you, like friends and family.

Remember: a good prank is one that makes everyone laugh, that doesn't break anything, and that doesn't hurt anyone! If your prank is going to make a mess, you need to be the one to clean it up afterward. If you're not sure if a prank is okay, ask a parent.

Without further ado, here are six fun, safe, and wacky pranks to try! Write down notes on how each prank went after you pulled it.

Prank Idea 1: Clothing Switcheroo

Here are two ideas in one! Version A: go into your target's closet and turn every single piece of their clothing inside out. Version B: swap the contents of a set of drawers or wardrobe so that everything is in a different drawer than it usually is.

How'd It Go? _____

Rate This Prank _____

Prank Idea 2: A Buggy Treat

Get a realistic-looking fake bug (and make sure it's clean). At your next meal, when your target isn't looking, sneak the bug onto or into your target's food!

How'd It Go? _____

Rate This Prank _____

Prank Idea 3: Funny Farts

A whoopee cushion is a classic prank item. Inflate one with air, slip it under a cushion on a sofa or chair, and have a good laugh when the next person to come along sits down on it and it makes a loud farting noise!

How'd It Go? _____

Rate This Prank _____

Prank Idea 4: Bubble Wrap

Sneak a big piece of bubble wrap underneath a rug or a doormat. The next time someone walks over it, they'll get a popping surprise!

How'd It Go? _____

Rate This Prank _____

Prank Idea 5: I'm Watching You

A pack of sticky-backed googly eyes has so much potential! Go around the house and stick a pair of googly eyes on all sorts of things, like kitchen appliances, fruit, soap bottles, plants, and more. Make sure that some items are tucked away to be found much later!

How'd It Go? _____

Rate This Prank _____

Prank Idea 6: All Tied Up

Tie the laces of several pairs of your target's sneakers together so that all the shoes are connected. When they go to grab a pair to put on, they'll be grabbing way more than just one pair!

How'd It Go? _____

Rate This Prank _____

What can travel around the world
while staying in one corner?

Where can you find towns
and cities but no people?

What has a neck
but no head?

What has many stories
but cannot tell them?

What has a tail but no wings and
yet can soar high in the sky?

What can you hold
but never give away?

What has many branches but
no trunk or leaves?

What can be cracked,
made, or told?

What has one head, one foot,
and four legs?

What can run but
not walk?

What is easy to get into
but hard to get out of?

What can be as big as a hippo
but still weigh nothing at all?

What begins with an "e" and ends with an "e" but only contains one letter?

What has thirteen hearts but no other organs?

What can you keep after giving it to someone?

What kind of band never plays music?

What needs to be fed but never wants to drink?

What can you serve but never eat?

WHAT CAN BE CRACKED OPEN BUT NEVER CLOSED?

HOORAY, YOU'RE HiLARiOUS!

We hope you had fun being the
best comedian you could be!

BETTER DAY BOOKS®

HAPPY · CREATIVE · CURATED

Business is personal at Better Day Books. We were founded on the belief that all people are creative and that making things by hand is inherently good for us. It's important to us that you know how much we appreciate your support. The book you are holding in your hands was crafted with the artistic passion of the author and brought to life by a team of wildly enthusiastic creatives who believed it could inspire you. If it did, please drop us a line and let us know about it. Connect with us on Instagram, post a photo of your art, and let us know what other creative pursuits you are interested in learning about. It all matters to us. You're kind of a big deal.

it's a good day to have a better day!®

www.betterdaybooks.com

better_day_books